To Ella,
Enjoy,

CW00404986

SHABBY

MADALYN

SHERWOOD-DAWSON

Mwh.

Dedicated to my sweet Shabby

ACKNOWLEDGMENTS

Firstly, I would like to thank my Mum for making this journey possible. Without her, none of this would have happened. She has helped me edit and publish this book. Not to mention the huge amount of time and financial support she has given. Next, I would like to thank my Dad, who has been so supportive, and inspires me to be better every day. He has been by my side throughout the making of this book which has helped to maintain my focus. Also, I would like to thank my neighbour and close friends, Michelle and Griff for letting my Mum and me gate crash their evening so that they could pass on their computer knowledge to help us format this book. Also, I would like to thank my very supportive Grandma. She has not only let us borrow her computer, but also helped bring this book together, giving me a few very good ideas regarding the formatting. Finally, I would like to thank my Best Friend, Bethan. She has stuck by my side throughout everything over this past year and without her, I honestly don't think I would have had the motivation to put pen to paper. I'm so glad that this book is now being published and it's all due to the massive support system I have had in my close friends and family.

CONTENTS

Part 1

Part 2

Part 3

SHABBY

Part 1

The Beginning

I have this distant memory of ten-year-old me, gazing nervously out of the dirty airport window. I could just about see a vague outline of the frightening aircraft, lined up next to each other like soldiers off to war. The sky was jet black like a vast area of nothing – stillness.

I glanced down at my watch. Sixteen minutes to three. Our gate wasn't due to open for another five minutes and I knew how Mum didn't like wasting time. She would arrive somewhere with not a second to spare – if not, then she was a few minutes late. It was the same for everything from school pick-ups to important job interviews. Dad, on the other hand, never missed a deadline and was never late for anything. They were polar opposites.

I was sitting back in my seat and looked over to Sam who was twiddling the red ribbon belonging to 'Black Bear'. That was his teddy – his best friend ever since I could remember and he didn't go anywhere without him. Not even the toilet! There is a two-year age difference between Sam and me. He only turned eight in July, which he didn't like as it made him one of the youngest in his class.

"How much longer?" I asked desperately. By this point my eyes were red and sore with tiredness.

"I'll go check the screens," Dad replied willingly. He read out a faint line of information about our flight: "Flight TOM612 from Gatwick to Sal, Cape Verde, gate open."

"Yay," I squealed as I jumped up out of my seat. I had been so excited about this holiday. My first proper holiday in the sun with my family by my side. I couldn't wait.

We approached the gate. One at a time, we showed our passports to the stern lady at passport control and before I knew it I was sat on the aeroplane pressing my nose against the small oval window. My stomach was alive with both excitement and fear as I never much liked flying. It was the thought of being thousands of feet above the ground travelling at hundreds of miles an hour. It went against everything I had learned in my science lessons. Everything about gravity and oxygen and the atmosphere. I didn't understand how we could be so high up and still breathe, how we didn't just suffocate. Or even how the plane didn't just fall out of the sky because of the lack of gravity. The thought of it made me feel slightly sick so I squinted my eyes shut and squeezed my mum's hand hard. The next thing I knew, the plane abruptly sped up and the g-force rammed me back in my seat causing uncontrollable tears to continuously roll down my plump, rosy cheeks. The thundering roar from the engines was deafening, it was aggressive like a large male lion defending its dinner. I snuggled into Mum burying my head in her arms and she gently stroked me down my back.

It calmed me. I always felt safe in her presence. Like nothing could go wrong. She's my guardian angel.

A few minutes later, I gingerly removed my head from my mum's arms and studied the land below. It was beautiful. The lights from the cars and houses sparkled like tiny, yellow diamonds. It resembled a whole new galaxy waiting to be explored. By then we were way up in the sky and the engines had calmed down. Somehow, I felt safe.

A few hours had passed and I had just finished my lunch: chicken dinner with roast potatoes and vegetables. I never understood how people didn't like aircraft food. Personally, I love it. Always have. Then again, I'd eat anything put in front of me if I could. But that's another story. We were halfway through the flight and things seemed to be going smoothly. I must have drifted off because later on I was woken up by the pilot announcing we were coming in to land. A rush of excitement whizzed round my body as the plane turned and the view of the small, bizarrely shaped island came into sight. It was like nothing I had ever seen before. The sea was aqua blue and glistening in the heat of the blazing sun. The island was dusty orange in places and the south coast was layered with brightly painted buildings and a wooden pier protruded into the vast tropical ocean. The nearer we came to the ground, the more detail I could see. It soon came to my attention that the colourful buildings were nothing like English houses. They were more like shacks – unfinished and run down. Eventually, I felt a sudden bump as we bounced onto the old runway. I looked outside. It was as though we had just landed on the moon. The shacks were out of sight now and all I could see was the hot, barren landscape.

Slowly but surely, the plane came to a stop and the doors opened. Instantly, I felt a flush of dirty heat attack my body and the wind was carrying the dust off the runway in mini tornados.

A short while later, after we had collected our luggage and paid for our visas, we were greeted by our taxi driver, an English man, named Dave. He told us he had previously lived in England with his wife and children and they had moved to Cape Verde to set up an English restaurant.

We soon approached Dave's truck which had 'Bailey's Bar' marked on the side and we placed our bags in the open boot. After a brief tour of the southern part of the island, we were dropped off at our hotel, the Melia Tortuga (the hotel we were staying at). As we struggled through the large polished glass doors with our suitcases, a kind Cape Verdean man, smiling from ear to ear, intervened and escorted us to the main reception, handing Mum and Dad a cocktail and Sam and me some crayons and colouring paper. Along with that came a delicious fruit mocktail that was a beautiful vibrant orange and red colour and was bursting with exotic flavours.

Eventually, we made our way to our apartment to have some downtime after our long journey. The apartment was lovely and had everything we needed: a TV, two decent sized bedrooms, a kitchen, living space, bathroom and a large balcony overlooking the pool.

A few hours later, after unpacking our stuff and changing into some more weather-appropriate clothing, we made our way down to the front of the reception where an old blue and yellow taxi quickly approached us. It had tape holding the left wing mirror together and I noticed a large dent in the front door. Hesitantly, we climbed in and requested to go to Santa Maria (the main town). Although we were tired, we were all too excited and wanted to explore.

It was only about ten minutes before we reached the large mass of coloured buildings. There were people with little pop-up shops selling handmade jewellery and hats, and small purses made from coconut shells. The atmospheric music from the restaurants echoed down the narrow back streets and everywhere you looked there were stray dogs and cats. Some were like no dogs I had ever seen before. However, almost all of them, were greyhound or whippet type dogs crossed with a Labrador, or something, I don't know. All I know is this made me nervous because as we walked down the narrow, cobbled stone back streets, we could hear dogs barking and fighting. Defending themselves. Trying to survive.

It was around 6:00 p.m. by then and we were beginning to get somewhat hungry. None of us felt comfortable enough yet to eat out as the surroundings were completely new territory. Consequently, we came across a small Chinese supermarket where we purchased some mini toasts and some jam and brought it back to the hotel. This went down a treat with a glass of orange juice before bed.

Love at First Sight

The next morning, we were up with the sun. Sam and I went out onto the balcony and stared longingly down at the crystal clear swimming pool. Kids being kids, we were desperate to go in. For Christmas, Father Christmas had brought us a giant, inflatable loggerhead turtle which we couldn't wait to put into action! Quickly, after making a cup of tea for Mum and Dad, we ran into the main bedroom where they were sleeping and begged to go in the pool. They agreed but Dad thought it would be a good idea to go out for breakfast first. This thought wasn't dismissed so after getting dressed and applying a generous amount of factor 50+ suncream we made our way down to reception where once again a yellow and blue taxi eagerly greeted us.

We were driven down the long stretch of unmarked road which divided the hotels from Santa Maria. The morning sun was gazing down onto the barren desert either side of us. Already, it was over 20 degrees C and it was only 10am.

"Three euros," the taxi driver said as he parked up next to a row of souvenir shops by the pier. Without hesitation, we thanked the man as Mum handed over four shiny euros, which included a tip.

It didn't take long to find somewhere to eat. A small ice cream parlour in the centre of the town caught Sam's eye because he spotted on the menu chocolate and banana crepe. As by now we were all starving, this sounded like a lovely option especially when we saw the freshly squeezed orange juice.

We were halfway through munching our pancakes when a little dog appeared by my side. He was different to all the other dogs. Instead of being large and handsome, he was rather small and shabby looking, with matted blond fur.

"Do not touch the dog!" Mum said to us, looking down, rather concerned at the sight. However, he looked old and like he hadn't been fed in days. He glared at me longingly with his shiny brown eyes and his little pink tongue hung neatly from his mouth. I couldn't resist. Discreetly, I dropped a bit of my pancake on the ground for him. And in seconds - gone. I repeated this a few more times until there was nothing but mushy banana and chocolate on my plate.

Eventually, we had to leave. We continued with our day: shopping, sunbathing and playing in the sea. We didn't get back to the pool as there was so much to see, in fact I don't think either Sam or I gave the pool another thought, but the whole time I couldn't get this little dog out of my head. It was as though I had been reunited with a long-lost family member.

"We should name him," I said to Mum as she was reapplying her suncream.

"Name who? What, you mean that little dog?"

"Yeah."

"Okay," she said with a smile on her face.

I tried to think of all the names that went well with his personality: Scruff, Hope, Scrat. Nothing was right! Until...

"I've got it!" I shouted.

Everyone looked at me.

"Shabby, we should name him Shabby!"

"I like it," Sam said.

"Yes, it suits him," added Dad.

"Shabby it is then," agreed Mum.

As the day began to come to an end, I started thinking: *Shabby is probably a stray which means he has no owner.*

"Can't we just adopt him," I said without really thinking.

"Absolutely not!" Mum said. "We can't just take random dogs home from third-world countries! It doesn't work like that," she argued.

"Please, there's not much harm in looking into it," I said desperately. So when we arrived back at the hotel, at my demand we sat in reception and researched if it was possible to take Shabby home. I think Mum agreed to pacify me as neither of us really thought it possible, but I needed to at least try. After a few minutes of looking, a website appeared on my phone: OSPA!

"Look at this." I showed Mum my screen and to her surprise, it was indeed possible to rescue dogs from Cape Verde. In fact, the shelter was only a five-minute drive away.

"Fine," said Mum, "tomorrow morning, we will visit this shelter and speak to the owner."

"Yes!" I squealed.

"Thank you, thank you, thank you!" I jumped up and began to joyfully skip back to the apartment. Mum shouted something to me about not getting my hopes up but I was too far ahead to take any notice.

Sure enough, the next day, Mum kept her word and we travelled the short journey to OSPA where we met a compassionate Italian lady called Dada. She welcomed us with open arms.

"We have a question for you," said Mum, "we understand we might be being completely ridiculous. However, we met a little dog on the streets and well, you see, we'd like to adopt him and we've named him Shabby. Is this possible?"

Dada stood there, looking blank for a second.

"Of course you can, my dears!" she said, suddenly raising her arms up in the air in excitement. I was so happy! It was almost impossible to think that two days ago we were just a normal family, on a normal holiday, buying normal souvenirs, and now we could potentially be going home with a dog.

"Why don't you come to the shelter with me and see our work, you can meet some of our rescued dogs? There are so many dogs that were once just like Shabby. Alone, starving and alive with fleas."

We all looked at each other.

"Please, Mum," I begged.

"Okay, okay, but when we get back we must search for Shabby."

"Yes, of course," I said.

Shortly after, Dada called for a taxi and we headed to OSPA. This taxi had a blanket of fur covering the dashboard. Dad said this was to stop it from cracking in the heat of the sun.

As we continued, a vast area fenced off with large metal panels, alone in the barren landscape, came into view. The main gates were painted orange and black and a sign said OSPA. I don't really know what I was expecting.

This shelter was very different from the high-technology, up-to-date shelters in England. This one was literally a bit of desert fenced off. It made me realise how lucky we actually are.

Slowly, the taxi came to a stop. We climbed out and in turn thanked the driver.

"Here we are," said Dada proudly, and as she opened the gate loads of excited dogs came running over to us. Jumping up and barking, they were trying to compete for attention. As I looked around, at the far end, there were rows of kennels. Not the sort you would find back at home. These kennels were made from any slight resource they could find. Planks of wood were used as the doors and old scrap bits of material were hung up to create some much needed shade.

External view of OSPA as we approached in the taxi.

We spent a long time at OSPA, chatting to Dada about the dogs. All these dogs had been rescued and were waiting for their forever, loving home. It made me feel sad and a bit guilty. We fell in love with a dog who was older. It would be ideal for him to enjoy what he had left of his life in OSPA. Sort of like a retirement, and Dada seemed to care deeply for every dog in her care. There were all these younger dogs too that if no one adopted them, would have to stay there for the rest of their lives constantly worrying about being the weaker dog and not getting into what could be a fatal fight. It was time to leave, we thanked Dada and headed back to the hotel. I couldn't stop thinking about the shelter and all those unwanted dogs. This was the first time I had experienced true poverty and in all honesty, it was a lot worse than I thought. At home, if we want water, we just have to walk over to a tap. Not here. Every month they have to pay to get a large barrel filled up with water and if it runs out before the month ends, tough luck!

Once we got back to the hotel, we grabbed a quick bite to eat before settling down for the night as we were all exhausted!

The next morning, we were up with the sun again. We had planned to meet Dave again as he was going to drive us to one of the local shanty town schools. This was something we all really wanted to do; we had planned this when we were back in England. We had brought pens, paper and some balls with us from home. This all seemed so insignificant so on our way there, we purchased a big bag of sweets to hand out to the children. I was really looking forward to visiting the school as not only is it a great way to learn about their culture but it would also give me something else to think about other than Shabby.

It was about a half-hour's drive to the school from Dave's restaurant, Bailey's. However, it only seemed like we were in the car for five minutes as the views from the windows were incredible, which was before the dirt coated the car in a thick layer of orange dust, completely obscuring our view, and the closer we got to the school, the poorer it got. The once unfinished, colourful shacks slowly turned into the secret dens my brother and I used to make when we were younger, out of mattresses and old sheets. The wind was blowing litter around like tumbleweed and children were walking about barefoot, trying to create their idea of fun out of sticks and plastic bottles. It was an eye opener to see such poverty when in my whole life, things had only ever been handed to me on a silver plate, well that's what my parents told me.

We soon pulled up outside a purple and green building with just holes with bars in the sides of the walls for windows and a fabric sheet for the roof, providing shade. As we entered the first classroom, the children swarmed round us like a herd of inquisitive calves. Each child desperately held their hand out for a sweet. It was heartbreaking. I noticed their eyes. So hopeful yet filled with sadness and despair, like they had given up. Yet, beyond the obvious, they were happy, so happy. They found pleasure from the small things in life and most importantly, they didn't take anything for granted. We spent a good hour with the children, getting to know their personalities and learning about their typical day. Most kids woke up, got dressed and came to school. They were provided with a basic breakfast and cleansing facilities. Once they had arrived in the classroom, as the average family couldn't afford so much as a toothbrush and a tube of toothpaste, each child had their own little pot with their name on and inside was a small toothbrush and toothpaste. These were lined up in rows like prisoners in jail cells. Each pot had been carefully and thoughtfully designed by its owner, and they added a spot of brightness to the corner of the room.

Soon our visit came to an end so we thanked the teachers for letting us stay before climbing back into Dave's truck. We were dropped off in the centre of Santa Maria as Mum had promised to let me get my hair braided in an African style. We walked for a while before finding a small orange building with a sign saying: The Hair Salon. As we walked through the beaded drapes two local ladies greeted us and told us what they could offer. I chose a braided style I liked which the lady soon did for me. Surprisingly, it hurt very little. Once it was done, my head felt so bare it was awesome! I kept nodding my head around like it wasn't attached to my body properly!

After my hair was styled, we made our way to find a restaurant for lunch. Sam and Dad (being the fishermen they are) spotted a seafood restaurant by the beach, which we ended up settling for. We quickly ate before beginning our search for Shabby. We continued looking for him into the next day, but still – nothing. We were beginning to worry as we only had two days left and on one of them we had planned to go swimming with lemon sharks, which Dad quite frankly said he was not going to miss because of one dog. This meant we only had the rest of that day (which was two hours) and the next day to find Shabby. I didn't know what I was going to do if we didn't find him. I would be heartbroken.

The next two hours felt pointless because we arrived back at the hotel having not seen a glimpse of Shabby. Where could he have been?

Before I went to sleep, I sat on the foot of my bed and prayed I would see him again. I was deep in thought when my mum joined me. She simply said, "If it's meant to be, we'll find him."

I looked up and smiled a blissful smile. But, beyond my dimples I was terrified. Terrified that we wouldn't find him. What if it wasn't meant to be? I slept on that thought, badly.

The Unexpected Other

The next morning we changed into our wetsuits ready to see the sharks. Although Shabby was the only thing on my mind, I was still very excited for this opportunity and I wanted to enjoy myself. I made sure I picked up my sufficiently charged waterproof camera, hoping to get some good shots of the sharks, and packed it in my bag. We made our way to a small minivan where we met an English man named Jonathan, he was involved in Explore Cape Verde, a company that works to promote biodiversity on the island and share the wildlife opportunities with tourists. Jonathan was the guy who ran some of the activities and I believed he was a marine biologist. Soon the van started and we drove to a small rocky beach which we hadn't visited before. We were all so excited getting out of the van. The thought of being within metres of real live lemon sharks was also very scary but that's what made it even more exciting! Once we were in the water, we began to see the tips of shark fins. A local Cape Verdean man came over to me; he must have noticed I was nervous being in the water up to my thighs. My nerves didn't bother him, he must have seen this many times before. He took my hand and deeper into the water we ventured. I was delighted to get a better look of the sharks and have him take some close-up photos with my underwater camera. I thought this was very kind of him, so willingly I let him.

It was amazing getting to swim with the sharks and as soon as I got back in the minibus, I couldn't wait to check my camera. The man had taken some pretty good photos. I was very pleased. However, the day was nearly over, and after we'd eaten, we went back to the hotel. Tomorrow was our last day on the island and our last chance to find Shabby. It was lovely at 7 am; we were already searching the streets. Dad, not being a dog person but a cat person, did not approve of how we were spending the last day of our family holiday.

"This is ridiculous! The last day of one of our few holidays we have together spent looking for a bloody dog!" he complained.

"Yeah, I'm bored! I want to go in the pool!" whined Sam.

"Please, we have to try," I begged. We continued walking. We hardly ate all day but it seemed like we had searched the whole island. There was nothing much left to do – or so it seemed – so we decided to go and speak to Dada and get her opinion on what to do. She said that if we didn't find him before we left, she would continue to look for him and email us if she saw him. This comforted me. Dad hadn't ever agreed to us adopting a family dog before. I know Mum had always wanted a dog, and she had corgis when she was growing up. We chatted about our day and made the decision, with Dada's permission, to visit OSPA once more. We all knew what was going to happen and agreed it wouldn't hurt to go and visit the shelter again. And, we knew this was to see if there were any dogs we would like, in case we didn't find Shabby, so we unanimously agreed, including Dad!

The dogs at the shelter weren't the types of dogs we had in mind, none looked like Shabby but all were different in their own way. They were barking and jumping like typical kennel dogs. We didn't know their temperaments. There was one dog, with ginger fur and curled ears, which Dad actually commented on. He said that she was very pretty but even after hearing Dad's views, Mum still disagreed.

"How can we take a dog from here over Shabby?" she exclaimed with a degree of sadness. Her sadness wasn't just for Shabby, it was for every dog there. We were just about to leave when they let the pretty ginger dog out of her kennel to run around. She was like a completely different dog. In the kennel with the other dogs, she was barking and growling and jumping at the old, worn wire fence. Nevertheless, when she was alone, running free around the shelter, she had a sense of confidence yet tranquillity. Her life was worth more than this. Watching her trot elegantly across the shelter made my heart melt. It was love at first sight and to my surprise, we all shared the same view.

We spent the rest of the evening with this dog (whose name was Larry) and it didn't take long before we'd all created an inseparable bond. This, however, changed everything.

"You are very welcome to take both dogs," exclaimed Dada.

"Okay, but suppose you don't find Shabby," said Dad, "what then?"

"Then you only take Larry," Dada said persuasively. "Look, at the end of the day, both dogs are going nowhere; they have no future on Sal, we have very little or next to no veterinary care facilities for the dogs, and neither of them have a happy, fulfilled life". She had a point. We looked at each other, our thoughts were unspoken but we knew we were all in agreement.

We chatted about the adoption possibilities before handing Dada enough money to cover the cost of Larry's microchip, vaccinations and some of the quarantine time. It was the best day of my life.

It was 5:30 p.m. by the time we left Dada's office and we decided to celebrate our last night by eating at the same seafood restaurant we ate at earlier during our visit. We arrived to find that other people clearly shared the same idea as there was a thirty-minute wait for a table. This was okay, we didn't mind. We decided to take a short walk down to the dancing waves. We stood there, staring out into the sea, the sea that was surging with laughter, while collecting up all our nervous thoughts.

Before we knew it, it was time to head back to the restaurant. We began walking up the sandy beach.

There were many dogs out that evening, they all gathered by the restaurants situated along the beach. I guess they were waiting for kind people to offer them food.

"Is that Shabby?" Sam said, pointing to a messy silhouette of a small scruffy dog. As I ran up the beach it was as though time was moving in slow motion. My heart was a train, pounding down the tracks and the closer I got, the more I realised that it was Shabby. I felt alive with excitement and relief. It was the same feeling you get on Christmas morning, when everything you've always wanted is sat there right in front of you. Sometimes there were things you didn't even know you wanted – needed so badly, until you had them. I threw my arms around him and held him close to me, keeping him safe. Before I knew it, I began to sob uncontrollable tears. There was a little wet patch of my sadness growing on the side of his neck. Mum walked over to me. She was crying too.

"Maddy, you know it's not the right thing to do, don't you? It's better to adopt Larry. We don't have a collar or lead. It's time – it's time to say goodbye."

She may as well have taken my heart and violently

ripped it out of my chest.

"Your table's ready," declared a waitress,

approaching us from inside the restaurant.

"Stupid dogs!" she said angrily as she shook a tea

towel in his face, trying to scare him away.

"No!" Dad bellowed."It's okay."

Looking confused and embarrassed, the lady

suspiciously turned around and went back inside.

Slowly, we followed.

"It's fine, he'll be there when we come back," said

Mum trying to comfort me. In the restaurant, I sat

whimpering my heart out like a lost puppy. As did

Mum. Sam was too young to truly understand so

was consequently not bothered. Dad, though,

moved the menu up over his face to cover his tears.

"We could still adopt both of them," he said quietly

to Mum, so I didn't hear.

"Yes! Yes, we could but Dada would have to find

him again," exclaimed Mum.

"Well, my love, if I've learned anything from being married to you for twelve years, it's not to give up."
"Are you ready to order?" said a Cape Verdean waitress standing at our table. I wasn't hungry. I didn't want to eat. Therefore, I ordered the chicken and when it arrived, I removed the bone, as if I had eaten the meat and wrapped the remainder up in a serviette for Shabby. Every now and then I peered round the corner to check he was still there. He was, curled up in a tight ball with one eye open, watching us, making sure we stayed close by. Once everyone had finished eating, we went outside to see him one last time. As we approached him, he stood up, probably feeling rather uneasy. I placed the chicken under his nose and spoke to him with soft words. Hesitating, his little black nose sniffed the chicken and before we knew it, he was chomping it down. There must have been sand clogging up his throat because he kept coughing, it was a horrible cough, the sort you would hear from a sixty-year-old smoker. Consequently, Dad went and fetched him an old, discarded, plastic bottle,

which we cut in half to make a bowl. We filled this with water to help him wash it down. We sat there for a moment, deep in thought until Sam finally spoke.

"I'm tired. Can we go back now?"

"Okay Sam," Dad answered.

"Could we make one stop on the way home – to see Dada and tell her we saw Shabby?" asked Mum.

"Please," I added.

"Alright, I suppose it wouldn't hurt," said Dad.

We arrived at Dada's office at 9:30 p.m. Was it too late? As we entered the office, Dada was just leaving.

"Hello, my friends!" she said.

"What brings you to my office at this time?"

There was a long silence.

"We found Shabby," Mum explained.

"Brilliant! Where is he?" asked Dada excitedly.

"Well, that's the problem. We didn't have a lead or collar with us so we had to leave him at the restaurant," Mum said.

"We took photos though," I offered, in the hope it would make a difference to us seeing him again.

"Okay. I see," said Dada, deep in thought. "Can you email the photos to the office email address please?" Dada asked, rapidly followed by "When do you leave for England?"

"We need to be at the airport in a few hours," Dad told her.

"That's fine. Once you leave, we will continue to search for Shabby and if we find him, we will email you. Are you still up for adopting both dogs?" asked Dada hopefully.

"Absolutely," I said, not giving any members of my family a chance to speak.

With that, we all hugged Dada, thanked her and said our goodbyes and made our way back to the hotel to pack. We made sure we had gathered all our belongings before climbing in a taxi for the last time. I didn't want to leave. It sounds weird but it was almost as if I had not only bonded with the dogs but also the country. It felt like home.

After waiting a short time at the airport, we boarded our plane and watched the beautiful island slowly disappear from sight. The further away we got from the island, the further away I was getting from Shabby and Larry, which was the worst feeling ever.

"Maddy," said Dad, halfway through the flight, "how would you feel about changing Larry's name?"

"I don't know. What to?" I said curiously.

"Something with a link to Cape Verde. Something significant," he exclaimed.

"I think that's a great idea," Mum said.

I tried to think of things related to the island. Together, we came up with a few ideas: Sal, Verde, Shanti and Ospa. They were all lovely names. But, the one that particularly stood out to us was Shanti. We all agreed this was the perfect name.

Three Days Later

We were home. We had told all our friends and family the news and, surprisingly, we had mixed responses. On the one hand, there were those who thought we were doing this amazing thing that was nothing but good. Although, understandably, others couldn't get their heads round why we wouldn't just adopt a dog from this country. Well, the answer to that is we simply wouldn't have done this. Our life was complete (or so we thought) and getting a dog hadn't even crossed our minds before. I came home from school three days after our return to find Mum sat on the sofa smiling. She looked ecstatic, over the moon with excitement. But then her facial expression changed completely. Her face went grey with sadness. I was confused.

"Mum, what is it?" I said, not really sure if I wanted to hear the answer.

"It's Shabby," she said, "they've found him."

"Well, isn't that a good thing?" I was bewildered.

"Yes, hun," she replied, "only, he's been diagnosed with bronchitis and chronic tick fever. He can't come to England."

I can't even put into words how upsetting this was for me – for us. I had only known Shabby seven days but it seemed like a lifetime. I loved him more than anything in the whole world. To have that taken away from me was like losing a limb. I felt numb.

"Think on the bright side," Dad said.

"You may not have Shabby. However, you can put all your energy into Shanti and make her feel welcome." And that's what I did.

After waiting a long five-and-a-half months for Shanti's arrival, which meant Mum and I had to drive to Amsterdam to complete, I learned to love her just like I loved Shabby and I created a friendship with her just like the one I had hoped for with him. This was great but considering Shanti's rough past, she was very fearful of pretty much everything: dogs, people, cars, bikes and even the sound of cutlery clanking together. If this wasn't bad enough, on top of that, she was aggressive towards most people and dogs. This made our life very difficult when it came to socialising although we found a way to minimise her aggressiveness and fear and create a loving family home for her. She was safe and happy and we all loved her regardless.

Part 2

Déjà Vu

There I was again, two years later after adopting Shanti, gazing out of the dirty airport window. But, this time, I was not nervous but excited. So excited. Mum and I had spent months prior to this washing cars and selling things online to raise money for OSPA. We also collected any items we thought the shanty town children and dogs in Cape Verde would like. We were going back. Revisiting the island that I hold close to my heart. I couldn't believe that after two whole years, I finally had the opportunity to go and see Shabby again. To visit the shanty town school. To relive the best time of my life.

A lot can happen in two years. Look at Shanti, for example. When she first arrived she was a nervous wreck. She would viciously attack any other dog or person that came near her whom she didn't know or trust. It had made life incredibly difficult when it came to socialising. However, now she is still fearful and doesn't like most dogs but is learning to trust people and has some doggy friends. When she plays with them it's like butter wouldn't melt (as my mum says.)

This time, it's just Mum and I going. Dad and Sam offered to stay at home and look after Shanti, which was a good idea as she would not cope with going into kennels.

As we boarded the plane to Sal for a second time, a rush of adrenalin shot straight through my body like a lightning bolt. It was so surreal. I had waited so long for this moment and now it was finally happening!

The plane ride was just as exciting, if not more so, as the first time we visited. When the plane turned around, over the southern end of the small island ready to land, all the beautiful memories I had suddenly all came flooding back to me. As we descended through the feathery clouds, I began to see the little coloured houses and the wooden pier protruding into the crystal ocean. The water sparkled in the light from the tropical sun.

Before we knew it, we felt the bump of the plane thumping onto the eroded runway. The doors opened and once again I felt the dusty humidity circling around me.

Just like before, we met Dave (our English taxi driver and the owner of Bailey's restaurant). At our request, he drove us straight to OSPA. We couldn't wait another day to see Shabby.

As the poverty-stricken kennels came into site, it felt like my heart grew ten sizes. All of a sudden, the memories I had of Shabby came flooding back to me. I didn't think I could love that dog any more. Yet, I proved myself wrong because I was falling in love with him all over again.

When we arrived at the shelter and knocked on the big metal gate, we were greeted by many dogs barking excitedly at the sound of our voices. We heard a lady named Maria Gloria welcome us. She was a local person who Dada employs to watch the dogs when she is not there. She came to open the gate. We gave her a big hug and handed her two suitcases filled with donations from our friends and family back in England, and there were also English chocolates for Maria and her family. This was to thank her from all the dogs and for her dedication to them.

Without hesitation, I ran to the bottom of the shelter where I saw Shabby's kennel. I slowly approached him and stroked his scruffy neck through the worn wire fence. He rubbed his head against me in appreciation and I couldn't have been any happier. It was like a hole in my heart had been filled. I had never loved anything or anyone as much as I loved Shabby and nothing was going to separate us again. I put my head close to his and whispered in his ear, "I love you". He then looked up with his affectionate eyes and that was it. I fell right into them. That was the moment I decided he was my best friend. Without him, I felt inadequate, incomplete, broken.

We spent a good few hours at OSPA, loving all the dogs, though Shabby in particular, before heading into Santa Maria, where we were going to be staying. It was nothing fancy. A self-catering apartment in the centre of the town which was close to the beach, shops and restaurants but most importantly, a five-minute taxi drive from OSPA. We checked into our apartment and changed into some lighter clothes. We then went into Santa Maria. As we were self-catering, we needed to get some food so we went into one of the small Chinese supermarkets. All around the island of Sal, there are small Chinese supermarkets run by Chinese people.

At first, I thought this was a little odd. But, after doing some research, I found out that the Chinese people are a community of entrepreneurial migrants who settled there in the 1990s to start retail shops. From them, we purchased local cheese, a pint of milk, a loaf of bread and some papaya jam. We also bought some fruit from a local lady selling it from a basket on the street.

After walking around for a short time, we headed to The Nautical Club. We knew we would find Dada there. The Nautical Club is further along the beach so we walked for about twenty minutes before arriving at the small blue beachside bar. The music echoed down the street. However, the stray dogs curled up by cars and at the base of trees didn't seem phased! As we walked onto the short decking that looked out onto the sea, we bumped into Dada. It was so nice to see her again after two whole years! We gave her a big hug and agreed to meet her the next morning.

We sat and enjoyed our food while listening to the live music being played by the locals. It was lovely to be reunited with an old friend. Dada was so kind and friendly, she made us feel very welcome. Before we knew it, it had got quite late so we decided to head back to get some sleep.

View from the balcony of our apartment.

Working Women

The next morning we were up with the sun and ready to go. We had planned to help at the kennels from 9:30 a.m.-4:00 p.m. so we had quite a long day ahead of us. Once we had changed into our old clothes and applied a generous amount of factor 50 suncream, we headed out to meet Dada. I loved the atmosphere in the morning. Local people walking around, going about their business, opening their shops. Dogs uncurling themselves from their sleep, the fishermen bringing in fish at the end of the pier and the sound of the local builders' metal hammers hitting breeze blocks as they build more houses, developing the country.

We headed around the corner to Dada's office where she was waiting in her famous green van. Mum got in the front and I climbed in the back. To my surprise, when I looked to my right I saw a large, furry face, smiling at me.

"This is Brownie Bob," Dada explained.

"He used to live at the shelter, although now he has recovered from his illness he is back on the streets. He loves us very much and sometimes just likes to come with us, back to his home."

"Bless him," Mum said. I then scratched the back of his neck, which he rather liked. Before the end of the journey, he was laid upside down on my lap. Still smiling.

Arriving at OSPA again, I was so excited and being greeted by some very lovely dogs made the whole experience even better. Obviously, I ran straight over to Shabby's kennel, where he was having his breakfast. There were two other dogs sharing his kennel with him. Gina and Linda. Gina was a gentle Labrador crossbreed and Linda was a calm female that had a deep scar above her left eye from a car accident. Shabby was slower at eating than the other dogs. His throat seemed sore and he struggled to swallow his food. Watching him struggle just made me want to take him home even more. To keep him safe. To be able to provide him with veterinary care and give him the retirement he deserved. While he was eating his breakfast I decided to take a walk around the kennels and get to know the other dogs. They were all so sweet. Being there made me realise that for every one dog rescued (anywhere in the world, not just Cape Verde) there are hundreds still suffering.

Later on, as Mum was cleaning the shelves and organising the medicines, Maria Gloria brought Shabby to me outside his kennel. I groomed him and loved him, giving him treats and scratching behind his ears, which he really loved!

Once Mum had finished organising the medicines, she came out to join me. She really loved this one dog, Roby. He was a similar size to Shanti and had the sweetest ears. They were pointy and made his face look super cute. Not to mention he had a little deformed nose, oh, and if that wasn't enough he had a deformed penis and urethra too, poor boy. Roby definitely needed a home of his own and more sophisticated veterinary knowledge than Sal had to offer. Roby's deformed nose, however, did not stop him from sniffing out all the treats in my pocket!

By the end of the day, I had really got to know every dog. Mio was a beautiful boy that had a problem with his back legs which made him walk funny but despite this, he still had such a happy soul. The puppies were new to OSPA. They had all been left to die but luckily Dada's team found them

and turned their little worlds into bright futures.
Then there was Pooky. He was the oldest dog there.
Blind in one eye. Yet, similarly to Shabby, all he
needed was love and affection. He had such a sweet
personality. There were so many more dogs like
Frankie, Rosalda, Rene, Frida, Gold, Rushton, Nina,
Hamburger – you get my point!

The day went by so fast and before we knew it, it
was 4:30 p.m. and we were starving. Before we left,
there was one thing I had to do first. Back in
England, we got Shabby a present. We managed to
buy him a personalised collar. It was a dark brown
colour and had 'Shabby' sewn on in a lovely bright
orange. I clipped the collar around his neck with the
writing facing up. He looked so smart. My heart
was beating as fast as the wings of a baby bird's first
flight.

It was about 5:40 p.m. by the time we got back to our apartment. We stood on our balcony and stared out to sea. Every wave that rolled back into the ocean seemed like it was drawing us nearer. We were both so tired. However, we couldn't think of a better way to spend our evening than heading down to the beach to enjoy our dinner while watching the sunset over the horizon.

We found a local restaurant that was cooking pork and chicken on a barbecue. The food was delicious. Served with rice and salad, and as it got dark some of the street dogs decided they wanted to join us. It was so lovely sitting outside feeling a dog's fluffy fur through my sandals, tickling my toes. Once we had finished our meal, we took a three-minute walk back to our apartment, where we decided to climb straight into bed as we had another long day ahead of us.

The next morning we were up early again, applying yet more suncream. We were heading off to OSPA again. This time we were only there for half a day as we were going to be writing in the log. The log is a book that keeps track of every dog's age, sex, personality and current health condition. This was done so that when it came to providing information to people who wanted to adopt, everything they needed to know was all there, up to date, in writing. We found another yellow and blue taxi that took us along the same long stretch of road that divides the big hotels from Santa Maria. It was only ten o'clock and already 28 degrees C. It was going to be a hot day.

Once again, we were welcomed by some very excited dogs, full of energy and ready for the day. Before we wrote in the log, there were three very young puppies that needed cleaning and feeding. They were so tiny and very sick. One in particular (the smallest) wasn't eating and consequently needed a bit more encouragement. Eventually, after giving her a dose of medicine and tempting her with small chunks of ham, we were able to persuade her to eat.

Next job, the log! We walked round the kennels with Dada showing us each dog and telling us bits about them. It was nice getting to know each dog better. I was beginning to form a bond with them, like they were friends – family even. The great thing about dogs is they don't judge you. You can talk to them and cry in front of them and they will still give you nothing but love and compassion. They truly are a man's best friend.

We left about 2:20 p.m. and it was 32 degrees C! Considering it was February and back at home the whole of England was at a pause because of the snow, it was very overwhelming so we felt some time in the pool was much needed!

We spent the rest of the day sunbathing and swimming. It was a lovely way to relax after three solid days of work (fun work, mind!). When evening arrived, we chose to head over to Dave's restaurant, Bailey's. It was Thursday, quiz night, so after a two-course meal we decided to take part. Well, what can I say apart from we-were-hopeless! One of the questions was 'who was the first reigning Stuart monarch?'. Our answer was Stuart Little! That was Mum's idea (obviously). Another was 'who ruled France in 1803?'. Again, Mum thought an appropriate answer was Francis France! Shows how much we know about history! Anyway, after sitting in Bailey's for a good two-and-a-half hours enjoying the atmospheric music and the sound of chirping crickets giving way to the velvety dark of the night, we decided to make a move. By the time we had taken a taxi back to the apartment it was midnight, so once again we crawled into bed and let our heads sink into our pillows, falling deeper and deeper into a heavy sleep, letting all the exciting events of the day reappear in our vivid dreams.

Desperate Souls

The next morning I was super excited as we were going back to the shanty town school. Along with all the generous donations for OSPA, we had also managed to collect, from some kind souls back in England, items for the school: more pens, paper, watercolour paint, pallets and paint brushes, also toothbrushes, toothpaste, clothes, shoes, deodorant and sanitary products. It may not seem like a lot. However, a little definitely does go a long way when you have so little. Some of those kids only got one small meal a day and had one or two sets of clothes. Despite this, they were still so happy as they didn't know any different. Each child had a smile on their face and the thing I loved most about those kids was they lived everyday as it came. Grateful for the little things in life and taking the bad things in their stride, like a hurdle in a race, they just had to figure out the easiest way to get past it so that they could carry on going.

We had arranged for Dave to pick us up at 9:30 that morning in his truck. We met him at Bailey's where he took us straight to the school.

The journey hadn't changed. As we drove past the little houses made from old mattresses, planks of wood and other materials, it brought back so many memories. The children were running around barefoot along the dusty, rocky ground and there was rubbish everywhere. Blowing around like leaves at the end of October.

Once again, we pulled up at the brightly coloured building to find the children hovering around us like seagulls at the seaside. As we entered, I remembered everything from our previous visit. The brightly coloured walls, the roof made from old fabric blowing around in the wind, the small hopscotch squares sprayed onto the floor in the corner. There were only five rooms in the whole school; the main courtyard, a tiny kitchen with one big saucepan cooking bean stew, two small classrooms and a smaller room that I think was for the older children and staff, oh and the toilets, so that may be six rooms if you count the bathroom. All the children followed us into one of the classrooms where we displayed our donations on a table so that everyone could see them. They were fascinated by what we had put in front of them. They reacted as if we had just given them millions of pounds-worth of gold. It was so lovely to see. Shortly after, it was their playtime. I helped hand out a small plain bread roll and a cup of water to each child before they went out to play. They were running around and touching my hair and my sunglasses and taking pictures on my phone. It was so cute.

I noticed some of the girls trying to do cartwheels in the corner. I was a national aerobic gymnast myself and I helped coach younger gymnasts of their age at home, so I went over to give them some help. Well, what can I say? Before I knew it, everyone was in a big circle with me in the middle and I was running my very own gymnastics lesson! Every child got involved and gave it a go and at the end they all clapped. It was a lovely, friendly atmosphere that made me realise how close they all were to each other, like one big family.

Reluctantly, after a really good day, it was time to leave. As we pulled away in Dave's truck, all the kids were waving to us. We waved back all the way along the long dirt road until the school was out of sight.

On our way home we made a quick stop to get some papayas and bananas from another lady selling fruit from a wicker basket, before heading into Santa Maria to get some lunch.

We decided to eat somewhere very special to us, the seafood restaurant on the beach. This was the restaurant where we saw Shabby on our last night before heading home in 2016 (two years before). The food in Cape Verde never fails to taste amazing! We ordered bruschetta and local cheese and papaya jam! For dessert, I had coconut pie, which also tasted so delicious!

Once our food had settled, we took a short walk over to the hair salon where I got my hair braided once again! This time I didn't get my whole head done. I just had four or five on the side. It looked very nice and then I felt like I blended in! Although, not too much because my bright, auburn, red hair still stood out like a sore thumb!

By now, it was around 4:00 p.m. and we headed back to the hotel where I went for an evening swim in the pool while Mum read a book. It was very peaceful. I could hear the birds chirping away to the sound of the crashing waves in the distance. I laid there in the water, like a starfish floating on the surface, thinking about my day, my trip. It was only just sinking in that I was actually in Cape Verde! I was in my favourite place in the world with Shabby and my mum. Things couldn't have been more perfect.

The next morning, I woke up naturally with the comforting warmth from the sun peeking through a gap in the curtains. We headed down to our favourite place for breakfast – the ice cream parlour. I obviously had my usual (chocolate and banana crepes and freshly squeezed orange juice) which I enjoyed very much. Mum had a large latte with hers which, I must admit, looked very appetising as it was served in a round glass jar and had the right amount of creamy froth on top.

After breakfast, we went down to the beach. We planned to have a lazy day playing in the sea and sunbathing. I headed straight to the sea while Mum laid out her towel on the smooth white sand, ready to lose herself in her thoughts. Although playing in the sea was fun, I sort of missed my brother. He normally kept me company. But I had no one. Never in my life did I think I would actually want my brother around. Normally, he is like an annoying wasp buzzing in my ear.

A while had passed and I started talking to a girl and her brother who were also on holiday. Her brother was a year younger than me and she was 16 (four years older than me). At first, I was rather short of words. What was I supposed to say to someone I had only just met? However, after a while I started telling her about Shabby and Shanti and before we knew it we were laughing and having a great time. It was like we had known each other for years.

Time flew by like a dancing butterfly and before we knew it the sky had developed a dusky glow and it was time to head home. Once again, I had another great day in my favourite place.

The next two days were spent at OSPA. We gave all the dogs their tick, flea and worm/parasite treatment. This consisted of going into each dog's kennel and rubbing a greasy liquid onto the back of their neck; this solution treated the ticks and fleas. It wasn't very nice to touch. The parasite treatment was a tablet the dog needed to swallow, so each dog received a tasty treat to disguise the tablet. It was a great experience.

I spent a lot of time with Shabby. We had a bond that was inseparable. Each day I grew to love him more and more and just when I thought that I couldn't possibly love him any more, my heart made a bit more room. I had never experienced true love before Shabby and now I had, it's something I never wanted to let go of.

Goodbye For Now

Unfortunately, the next day was our last day. We went to OSPA to say our goodbyes. I spent the majority of the time with Shabby as I didn't know how to leave him. I was just about to turn around when Dada approached me.

"He's much happier with you, you know."

I looked up at her, a tear rolled down my cheek and dropped off my chin.

"Plus, his health has improved loads in the two years he's been with us," she explained.

Mum joined us and smiled. "I've been talking to your Dad by text for a few hours." She handed me her phone and allowed me to read her messages.

I couldn't believe what I was reading! I was speechless. I had a beaming smile that went from ear to ear and I just stood there. There was a long silence.

"Thank you, thank you, thank you!" I squealed, running over to Mum and hugging her tightly.

"He will need to stay with us until he has had his vaccinations," Dada explained, "and then, we will figure out a way to get him home, with you, where he belongs."

I was so happy... ecstatic... overjoyed! There isn't even a word to describe how happy I was. But, it was a bittersweet feeling. It was time to leave. We said goodbye to Dada and Maria Gloria and all the dogs at OSPA before getting into a taxi that would take us to the airport.

Unexpectedly, we got to the airport to find our flight had been cancelled until the next day because of the snow back home. We were redirected to an all-inclusive hotel that the airline paid for. The hotel was lovely, it had lots of small holiday lodges, three amazing pools with bridges and swim-up bars and lots of little gift shops. That evening, we simply enjoyed the facilities at the hotel and decided on an early night.

Day nine (our extra day) was amazing! We went with Dada around the streets of Santa Maria and Palmeira (another nearby town) to take any sick or injured street dogs to OSPA. Dada's green truck was well recognised in Palmeira. As soon as she pulled up, floods of people hovered around it with sick dogs that need treating. Sometimes all they needed was some medicine or something simple like a trim of their nails or a dab of iodine on a wound. However, other times, it was more serious. We ended up taking four dogs to OSPA that day. One had open wounds and was severely underweight, another appeared to have broken bones somewhere from the waist down and couldn't walk and the other two were covered in mange and needed some consistent nourishment. Mange is a highly contagious skin disease found in dogs, caused by the Sarcoptes scabiei mite. These mites burrow through the skin causing intense itching and irritation. It's the scratching that causes the majority of the animal's hair to fall out. It certainly is disgusting and it smells gross too!

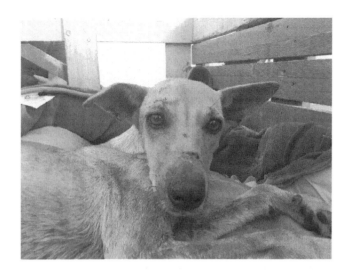

Shortly after, we headed back as we needed to see if there were any updates on our flight. We approached the hotel desk and asked about our flight. The lady handed us a piece of paper which had a list of flights and the days and times they were leaving. We scanned down the list until we saw our flight number. It said that our flight was cancelled again until the next day, which meant we had another free day to spend at OSPA!

When we woke up the next morning, we realised it truly was our last day; the snow had melted in the UK, flights were once again taking off from Bristol

Airport. The thought of leaving Sal made me feel sick. Cape Verde felt like my home and the thought of leaving it again saddened me.

We caught a blue and yellow taxi to OSPA for the last time and were greeted by all the dogs with their lovely, excited personalities also for the last time, although I wasn't seeing Shabby for the last time. I gave him a gentle hug as a tear ran down my dusty, warm cheek. I sat on the dirty floor next to him, savouring his smell and the feel of his fur on my arms. I was lost deep in my love with Shabby and I wanted this moment to last forever. "Come on," Mum said abruptly, interrupting my lost distant thoughts. "We have a plane to catch." I whispered into Shabby's ear, "I promise I will see you again very soon, don't ever forget I love you," as I reluctantly stood up.

It wasn't goodbye, more like goodbye for now. Even though I knew I was going to see him again, I still had to wait many months and that in itself was enough to make me cry. I sobbed uncontrollably as I walked away from his kennel.

Mum put her arm around me, "We will see Shanti later today, she will have missed you." This made me think of home, I had missed Shanti, however, time was moving in slow motion and every step I took away from Shabby, tore my heart even more than the last. I loved him so much. I still do, and I had to focus on the fact that the months would fly by. I would see him again, I knew that. And even though I couldn't be with him right then, we would still be looking at the same sky, the same ocean and I would always see him in my heart.

Part 3

A Long Road Ahead

Most nights I would stare up at the sky and talk to Shabby in the hope that he would hear me. He was nearly three thousand miles away yet he always felt so close. So close to my heart that he could probably hear it beating. One beat after another like the hands on a clock symbolising the movement of time, the movement of time which seemed to be moving so slowly. Every day was agony. Shabby had to stay in Cape Verde for many months as he needed to meet the government's requirement for rabies status, which takes a minimum of four months. It was such a long period of time, it felt like a lifetime.

Finally, after what seemed like many decades, the time had come. Shabby was ready to fly to England.

Months, weeks and then days passed and every second I was getting more and more impatient. But, when we started buying his bed and toys and sorting out the flight paperwork, that's when it actually sunk in that it was really happening.

About three months prior to that, we had all just had our hearts broken by Shabby, yet again, as we found out he'd failed his rabies tests and was unable to fly. This was because he was not producing the right amount of antibodies that were needed to meet the requirements. We were told by Dada that Shabby was very distressed when his blood was taken, which was why we were reluctant to have him take the test again. On the one hand, he was my best friend and I would do anything to hold him close to me again but, on the other hand, we didn't want to put him through the stress again if he was going to fail.

We were reassured, however, by the vet who said that one in three dogs fail the test first time but that decreases quite significantly the second time. That is what made up our minds. We decided to have the test done again knowing that if he failed, it wasn't meant to be.

Once again, we were waiting. Waiting for news that would change our future. All we could do was wait. Five more weeks had passed when I came home from school one day to see an envelope, addressed to me, propped up on my dressing table. Curiously, I tore open the seam and slid out a small blue card. On the front, in swirly black print, it said: *Sometimes you have to wait for the storm to pass before you can dance in the rain.* I instantly knew what the card was for. I lifted up the top half to see my mum's handwriting:

Shabby has passed!

Those three words were the best three words I had ever read in my entire life. I felt so relieved. After months of waiting around there was finally something for me to look forward to, Shabby could now legally leave Sal. We just needed to wait the required 90 days following his positive rabies test. Tears of joy rolled down my face.

We only had to wait three months after that, which for some reason went so fast, and before I knew it the time had come when I would walk into the kitchen and hear Mum on the phone to pet transport companies and airlines. I was kept out of the loop somehow. Yet, what I did know was that Shabby was going to fly from Cape Verde to Portugal, swap planes and then fly from Portugal to England. This was for a few reasons but the main one was to break up the journey for him so that it didn't put his respiration under stress. Mum didn't bore me with all the details as she was having a bit of trouble with transport from the Portugal flight to the UK. All I knew was it was a long, tiring process that was a worry for Mum and made her very stressed.

It was an ordinary Thursday evening and I had just got back from school.

"How was your day, Maddy?" Dad asked.

"Good," I replied. You know, the usual response to that much overused question.

"Shabby's in Portugal," said Mum, smiling at me waiting for a response.

"Okay, we had a science test today and…" Wait, what did she just say? It suddenly occurred to me what that meant.

"Shabby's in Portugal. He flew from Cape Verde last night and he's supposed to fly here, to Heathrow tonight. However, the flight company doesn't claim to have the right paperwork and there is no one to guide me," Mum said. I could tell the whole thing was very aggravating for her.

"The airline said there is a chance he might make the flight out on Monday. Nevertheless, the Portuguese vet is concerned. She doesn't think Shabby's breathing will be up to another flight," she added.

"I am waiting on an email from the pet carrier to clarify if Shabby will be able to get on the next flight tonight and, if not, which is unlikely, I have come to the decision that you and I will get in the car and drive all the way to Lisbon, Portugal, to pick him up." My jaw dropped!

"How long would that take us?" I asked, my voice all high pitched with excited shock.

"I don't know for certain. It will be a very long drive. Maybe four days, but we will know more later tonight regarding the Heathrow flight." Mum was clearly worried and looked tired from the worry. "If Shabby doesn't board the Heathrow flight, by tomorrow evening we will know what we are doing, so just in case, while you are at school tomorrow I will go and get my car checked, and I will organise European breakdown cover and check I'm insured to drive across four countries."

It was obvious to me that Mum was troubled by the frustrating situation we had found ourselves in and clear that she was apprehensive about the possibility of driving to Portugal to collect Shabby on our own. Looking back, what choice did we have? If we waited until the Monday, there was a chance his health would deteriorate and he would be refused a flight yet again. We didn't know what the problem was so planning was difficult. Everything was very uncertain.

I went up to my room to reflect on what had just
happened.

So many thoughts were rushing through my head.
What if we crashed, what if we got lost, what if
Shabby didn't travel well in a car? But then I
thought, what if none of those things happened?
What if we got back to England and he was safe? I
could walk him to the shop and cuddle him at night
and wake up in the morning to his happy little face.
All this made it worth it. We had to go for it. We
had to try.

Reluctantly, I went to school the next morning. I sat
in class listening. Not to the teachers' faded voices,
but to my heart. I was so overjoyed but terrified at
the same time. Shabby was coming to England. My
dream was slowly but surely turning into reality.

At the end of the day, after getting off the bus, I ran
home to see if there was any news. Mum told me I
was to go to gym as normal and when I got back she
would probably have an update on what was
happening. Great – more waiting! It seemed like all

I was doing was waiting. It was getting very disheartening.

I got back from gym at around 6:30 pm and once again I ran straight through the door to see if Mum had any news. She had.

"Right, Maddy. I would like you to go to bed now as we are getting up again at midnight and driving to Portugal," Mum explained.

Oh my! I was so excited. I didn't know how to react so I just stood there beaming from ear to ear. It didn't really seem true. After all this anticipation, waiting and heartbreak, actions were finally underway.

Shortly after, I went upstairs to get ready for bed. I also packed a small rucksack containing some essentials, such as a toothbrush and toothpaste, my phone and car charger, some CDs and lots of pillows and blankets. I was also responsible for putting a bag together with all Shabby's things. I packed some chopped chicken, a portable water bowl, a few coats for Shabby and a harness and lead. The only thing left to do was to go to sleep.

The next thing I knew, Mum was gently patting my shoulder and whispering my name. I looked at my phone, 11:40 pm. We had twenty minutes before we needed to leave so feeling very excited, and slightly nervous, I jumped out of bed and put some comfy clothes on. After all, I was going to be cooped up in my mum's car for four days! I grabbed a pair of grey jogging bottoms and a dark red baggy t-shirt before cleaning my teeth. I went downstairs to find Mum saying goodbye to Shanti. She was hugging her tightly.

"Goodbye, my sweet girl," she said, crying into her fur.

"I'm sorry. You were always enough. I love you so much and I am being so selfish and ridiculous. I'm sorry."

She seemed so upset and scared, it made me realise actually how crazy this was.

"Grandma and Michelle will look after you. I will be back soon." Michelle was our neighbour who had a big heart for every dog. Shanti had accepted Michelle like her second mum and she was right behind us every step of the way. We knew we could count on her. Mum turned around to find me standing in the doorway.

"Ready?" she said, wiping her eyes.

"Let's go!" I replied.

The Adventure

I hopped in the car with one of my protein porridge pots for breakfast because I had run out of time to eat at home. Before I knew it, I was sat in the passenger seat next to Mum. Dad and Sam had gone on a short fishing trip so that it was less overwhelming for Shabby when he first arrived. Of course that plan hadn't worked out but the boys still went on the trip regardless.

As we drove away, I was feeling all kinds of emotions. I couldn't decide if I was scared or excited or just tired. Maybe all three.

When we turned onto the motorway I had this long feeling of dread and regret. What were we doing? Were we insane? Mum looked at me as if she knew exactly what I was thinking. She reached for my cold, pale hand and held it tight to reassure me that things were going to be okay. Mum and I had a really special friendship and although I was terrified for our long road ahead, I trusted she would keep me safe. That was always the way with my mum. Nothing ever went wrong as long as she was by my side.

We only stopped once for a toilet break and a refuel during the five hours we were in the car; that was before arriving at Folkestone to get on the Eurotunnel. It was not the first time I had been on the Eurotunnel. I had travelled on it twice before. The first time was to collect Shanti from Amsterdam when she first arrived and the second was on a school trip to Belgium. Dad said I was very lucky as some people, including him, don't ever get to ride it. I guess it is pretty cool. You drive onto a train which takes you through a very long tunnel (that is built under the sea) to get to France. It defies logic!

It only took thirty-five minutes on the train to reach France. It was really strange. Before we got on the train, Mum was driving on the left. However, when we arrived in France, we were on the other side of the road. This meant Mum needed to think extra hard when it came to things like roundabouts. By that point, we were still feeling pretty good. Not too tired.

As we drove along the smooth, vast motorways in France, the sun was coming up over the horizon and stained the sky a vibrant orange. It was beautiful. The only downside about the luxurious roads covering France was that every few hours we would come across a toll where we needed to pay some money. The amounts varied, but sometimes it was as much as €36! This soon added up.

We continued driving all day with very few stops. We noticed, at about two o'clock in the afternoon, that it was 27 degrees C. This was crazy. It was October!

Our first proper rest stop of the day was at a lovely woodland services. There were nice little parking spots hidden away under some trees. It was six o'clock and we were so tired. Mum had been so anxious for Shabby that she hadn't had any quality sleep for the last three nights, so consequently had a thirty-minute power nap, which seemed to leave her feeling rather more energised. We set off again with

thirteen hours before we would arrived in Portugal.
We were ready for any obstacles that came our way.
It was two o'clock in the morning before we reached
Spain. We didn't realise how big France actually
was because it seemed to go on forever. Well, I
suppose it is about double the size of the United
Kingdom. We calculated eight hours and thirty-six
minutes until we would arrive at the Portuguese
border. This motivated us to keep going, even
though we were exhausted. Already, I had gone
twenty-six hours without any proper sleep. I could
now see why the US military used sleep deprivation
as a torture method up until 2009. I was so
physically exhausted that someone could have
stapled my eyes open and I still would've fallen
asleep.

Spain was so amazing. It was as though we were in
the middle of the savannah. The road was lined with
sloping red rocks holding back a vast, dusty stretch
of land. Land that was covered in cacti and African-
style trees that were growing on a slant. I had
learned about places like this in my geography

lessons and now to actually be there was pretty
amazing. I mean, it's not every week you drive for
four days, across four different countries!

Part way through Spain we made another stop at a
services. I went into the toilets to freshen up. I was
only in there for ten or fifteen minutes when Mum
found me. She was all panicked and tense.

"Maddy! I thought I'd lost you!" she said in relief,
hugging me rather tight. "I looked everywhere for
you and I thought you had been kidnapped!"

Granted, she was very tired, but, very dramatic. I
just laughed and reassured her that I hadn't been
kidnapped!

Shortly after, it was time to get back on the road. In
north Spain, there were a lot of long tunnels through
mountains. Some were very long causing the car to
be in complete darkness for a few minutes. It was
very strange! The sun was looking down on us.
However, the sky was grey and gloomy from storm
Lesley.

After what seemed like a lifetime of driving, we
were passing signs for Portugal! We were about an

hour away from the border and both Mum and I were as tired as a middle-aged mother with newborn triplets!

As we entered Portugal in the early hours of Sunday morning we were greeted by a range of large mountains that cast a murky shadow over the car (similar to those that sagged under my eyes). The mountains were rocky and steep and gave off a very eerie vibe. The roads quickly became more and more submerged in the busy landscape, swallowing the car into the heart of the crags.

The closer we got to Shabby, the faster my heart was beating. We had one hour and fifty-one minutes left and each minute that passed made me even more impatient as by now I was so eager to get there. Mum claimed to be at her most tired and on top of that we were running out of food and water in the car. We would have stopped but the kennels closed soon and we had no time. We had no choice, we had to push on.

Driving through Lisbon was very confusing. Almost as bad as London. Interestingly, it had large bridges

and tunnels covered in graffiti. It was quite amazing looking at all the different forms of artwork sprayed onto the walls of buildings. We drove under an enormous viaduct which was so spectacular. The views from the top must have been incredible!
We went from hours away to minutes, and the last fifteen minutes went slower than a three-legged dog on tranquillisers walking uphill! We drove over a large red bridge hovering over a vast blue patch of ocean. To our left was a big green statue, which reminded me of the Statue of Liberty, and to our right was the highly populated city. It looked like someone had just splattered a load of colour onto a blank canvas. The sun was shining. It was the perfect day.

In Love

Finally, after more than thirty-six hours of driving we had arrived. We turned up the narrow drive of the kennels to see Shabby. There he was, more beautiful than ever. I can't even explain how in love my heart was. I can't put it into words. Imagine being reunited with your best friend. The only person that you can truly trust, the only person that will never judge you and the only person that loves you just as much if not more than you love them. Imagine that but times ten. That's the only way I could possibly begin to tell you how much I loved him.

I got out of the car and ran towards him. Suddenly, I didn't feel tired any more. I was too in love. I wrapped my arms gently around him and kissed his neck multiple times. He pressed his scruffy head against my arm, his dry nose touching me. As I scratched the outside of his ear, Shabby leaned into my arm and rested there for a while. I felt his relief as he breathed gently on my arm. He seemed so at peace. He appeared to remember me. I had waited so long for this moment. Shabby was coming home with me. His body felt warm and he smelt beautifully familiar. Neither of us could have been happier to be reunited in each other's company. Nothing was going to separate us now. I promised Shabby, as I had done many times before, nothing would stop me loving him. There wasn't any other thing in the entire world that I loved more. At that moment, Shabby was my world.

We collected Shabby's things and carefully put him into the cosy fabric dog crate in the boot of the car. There were pillows and a blanket and a bone filled with peanut butter for him. He didn't seem to be stressed at all. Just happy, so happy and thankful. Mum and I refilled our water bottles and used the toilet at the kennels. Then, it was that dreaded time to turn around and do the full journey again. It was the worst feeling. Yet, I didn't care. I didn't care how long it took us to get home. I was just so grateful that my dream was finally coming true.

A few hours into our drive home, after I must have fallen asleep, I was woken abruptly by Mum grumbling to herself crossly while trying to work the satnav. We were parked in a small lay-by on the side of the road.

"Are we still in Portugal?" I asked, somewhat confused. The evening sun was shining in my eyes

"Yes. Unfortunately, we are. The satnav had sent us south instead of north and we would have nearly been in Spain by now, but we need to drive at least another four hours north as we are pretty much at Faro, on Portugal's south coast!"

I was in shock! Why did this happen to us? How? Anyway, we managed to work the satnav and began driving north. This was the only mistake since leaving Somerset – Mum hadn't done too badly so far.

We kept driving for many hours. At last, after a long day, we crossed the Spanish border and found a services to stop at. By that time it was dark and we were at what we thought was our most tired. My skin was pale and I felt very faint. My eyes were shutting and I just wanted to lose myself in a deep sleep. Goodness knows how Mum felt. At least I was able to catnap while we were moving.

About an hour later it was time to wake up. We walked Shabby around the outside of the services and made sure he had a drink and some food. When we returned to the car, I spent a few moments cuddling Shabby while Mum was taking some pictures of us. Suddenly, he pushed his wet nose up against my ghastly cheek, giving me the best, most gentle kiss I had ever felt. Mum managed to capture it on camera. It was a very special moment. We then put Shabby in the car to rest while we briefly went inside to use the toilet and get a drink and a snack. As we walked in, we instantly felt rather intimidated. It was a typical Spanish bar. Local men were at the bar cheering at the bullfighting on the TV. I hated watching the bullfighting, so I grabbed my hot chocolate and made my way back to the car with Mum close behind.

We were back on the road for about twenty minutes but despite the earlier stop, Mum was still too tired to drive. She found it particularly difficult to drive during the dark hours. I guess all her body wanted to do was sleep. She was swerving all over the road and people were flashing their lights at her. At one point I'm pretty sure she said she could see purple goo coming out from the side of the road! Maybe I was hallucinating too – I think you get the message. Mum was very, very tired.

After our pit stop, we were ready to go again. With eleven hours till we reached the border dividing Spain from France, things couldn't have been better! Eleven hours slowly turned to ten then nine and before we knew it, we were crossing the border. We stopped at the first services we could find to let Shabby have a quick stretch of his legs and for us to grab a drink and use the toilet. However, we were going to struggle to meet our Eurotunnel time so we had to make it really quick.

As we turned out from the services, we got rather lost. We managed to make our way onto the motorway. Something felt wrong and we didn't know what it was until Mum noticed that all the signs were facing the wrong way! Suddenly we realised that we were driving the opposite way down the motorway! Luckily, for that moment there were no cars on the road so we quickly turned around and made a sneaky escape! Looking back, it was very dangerous (and funny!).

After racing the clock to get to the Eurotunnel in time, we missed it by minutes and had to pay £68 to travel on the next one. The pet check-in was closed, which meant we had to find the all-night check-in. We approached the small cabin which had a large sign out the front that said: 'Overnight pet check-in'. The automatic doors slid open as we approached. Shabby was eager to get inside as he was probably very scared and needed somewhere to curl up and feel safe. The small cold room was very dark since there were no lights in there, and at the far end stood a stern lady protected by a thick layer of glass. We handed her Shabby's documents, which she stamped and handed back to us. We walked back to the car before driving over to the Eurotunnel. We got onto the train and after an unimaginably long and exhausting drive, we could finally relax. We knew that after the Eurotunnel, we only had a five or six-hour drive back home.

Mum was particularly relieved to make it to the Eurotunnel; her car was ten years old. If the car had broken down on the wrong side of the water we would have had a replacement car until ours was fixed, which meant we would not be able to travel back on the Eurotunnel in the replacement car but, instead, as foot passengers. The problem with that is you can't take dogs on the Eurotunnel as foot passengers.

Mum was relieved to say the least.

We slept throughout the whole ride back in the tunnel, which was a much needed and much deserved thirty-minute nap. England, the other side, was the worst part of the whole trip.

The motorway was closed, meaning we were diverted, which made us completely lost. Not to mention the fact that we were both zombies by this point. I was so tired, I couldn't even speak. Mum, drunk with fatigue, could hardly keep her eyes open and was swerving all over the road. I think Shabby felt a little left out because when the car fell quiet, he began to snore rather loudly. It was so funny. At times, Mum and I couldn't stop laughing! I guess when you're that tired you laugh at the strangest things.

Finally, after many hours, we managed to reach a place that seemed familiar to us. It was such a relief.

Turning off the motorway into our home town was one of the best feelings ever and I was so excited to begin my future with Shabby.

During the last few hours of our journey, to keep us awake, Mum and I started to list ways to fundraise for all Shabby's vet bills (as we knew there would be a lot to come). We came up with car washing, cake sales, a public online funding page and car boot sales. This was just a bit of fun to keep us awake but was going to be essential in helping Shabby back to full health!

We pulled up in our driveway just before eight a.m. on the Tuesday morning. All my friends that live near me were heading towards the bus stop ready to start another long day at school, but I was in no fit state to go. On her way to the bus stop, my best friend Bethan stopped to meet Shabby. She was almost as excited as I was and she too could not wait to get to know him. I stayed at home that day to sleep and be near Shabby. Despite my tiredness, it was one of the best days ever.

We made Shabby a little space just for him in the
lounge; this was to give him his own space to
recover from the journey and where he could feel
safe as everything was unfamiliar to him. He might
have never walked on grass or carpet before so we
needed to give him some time to unwind.

We hadn't introduced Shanti and Shabby yet
because we knew that Shanti wouldn't accept
another dog right away, even if it was her old
kennel friend.

I stayed with Shabby most of the day, loving him and comforting him. I noticed that his breathing was still bad. He would grunt and gag like he had something stuck in his throat. I spoke to Mum and she reassured me that he had been troubled by this snuffle for a long time and believed if it was anything serious he wouldn't have had clearance to travel.

That night I went to sleep so happy. I laid in bed and smiled. I couldn't stop thinking about Shabby. The fact that for nearly three years I had been longing to bring that little dog home and now he was downstairs snoring away in my living room. It was as though I was dreaming and I didn't want to wake up.

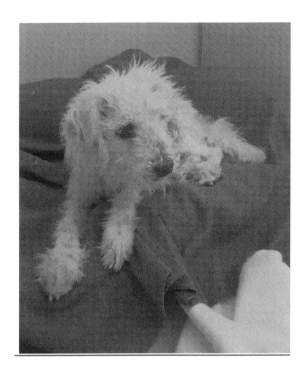

The End

The next morning Mum came into my room and sat on the side of my bed. She told me that Dad and she had sat with Shabby for a while that night, watching him since she was concerned with his breathing. She told me that at about 1:00 a.m. she decided to take him to the vets to get some help for his noisy breathing or some medication. They had kept him in for observation for the rest of the night. I was a bit worried.

"He's going to be fine," Mum said reassuringly. Trusting Mum's words, I continued getting ready for school before receiving a kiss on the head from her as I was going out the door.

"Try not to worry, Hun. Shabby will be home when you get back from school," she said confidently.

"Okay!" I shouted as I ran out the door to meet Bethan. Bethan knows me better than anyone and if there was anything I'd learned from knowing her for so long, it was that she always knows best! So I told her everything on the bus. She gave me a hug and said how lovely she thought Shabby was.

"Tonight I am coming to yours and we are going to binge-watch Netflix with popcorn and Shabby. Okay?"

"Sounds great!" I replied, and we both giggled as we arrived into school.

That day was pretty boring. I'm not going to lie. Lunch rolled around and it was the best feeling ever, knowing that I only had one period left before I could see Shabby.

I was sat at the table bragging to three of my friends about how amazing he was. I could tell by their faces they were getting bored but I couldn't help it. I had never been so happy in my life. Until something happened...

One of the teachers approached our table asking if anyone had seen a 'Madalyn Sherwood-Dawson'. Hesitantly, I raised my hand.

"You need to go and find your brother and the both of you need to make your way to the office. Your mum is here," he said, looking annoyed he had to come and find me. My heart was racing. Shabby was the first thing that jumped to mind. I felt sick.

"Why?" I asked.

"You have an emergency dental appointment. Hurry," he replied, and then walked away.

I slowly brought my eyes down to meet Bethan's. She looked just as concerned as me.

"I have no emergency dental appointment," and a fearful tear dripped off the end of my nose.

The whole table went silent. I stood up, pushing my chair out behind me. I started to run to the office, not waiting for my friends who were trailing behind me. Suddenly I didn't care about them. I didn't care about anyone or anything apart from Shabby. I knew something was wrong. I could hardly run. Everything around me was a blurry image moving in slow motion and I thought my legs were going to collapse from beneath me.

I began to walk. Through the office doors, I could see Mum. Her eyes were red and puffy and her shoulders fell low. As I entered the room, she started to sob.

"Sit down," she said, through her cracking, fragile voice.

"You are aware that Shabby went to the vets. Well, they did some checks and..." more tears fell down her cheeks, her voice breaking into a million pieces.

"Mum," I said, urging her to go on.

"They found cancer in his nose. It's the worst they've ever seen. We have to let him go." It took me a while to process what she had said. But then it clicked.

I began to cry uncontrollably. Tears just kept coming from my eyes and dripping onto the floor. What she had said was the equivalent of ripping out my heart and squeezing it so tight that I couldn't breathe. Part of me wanted to run out of air. I didn't care about life. I suddenly felt useless. I had nothing left to fight for.

This wasn't the plan for Shabby. His story wasn't supposed to end this way. My tears were black with mascara and I just wanted to give up. After everything we had been through to bring him home, it was the worst possible outcome. We brought ourselves out of the reception and got in the car. "He is under general anaesthetic now," Mum said, "I want us to be with him at the end, he needs us to be with him and to know how much we love him. The vet is waiting for us."

I said nothing. I could not speak.

My eyes and nose were sore and just as I was catching my breath, I heard Sam in the back of the car breaking his little heart. He didn't know what questions to ask first. Sam never cried. He was a confident year seven without a care in the world. As we pulled up at the vets, it felt like everyone was staring at the black, wet stains down my cheeks. The space surrounding us as we walked towards the vet's entrance was a blur. We walked through the door (still sobbing.) Other loving pet owners were sitting waiting for their turn to see the vet. I don't know how many people were waiting but it didn't matter.

Nothing mattered more than Shabby. The vet showed us through to the room at the back where

Shabby was laid. The room was small and so quiet. Shabby was laid on what looked like a theatre table, covered in the blanket Mum had taken in with him earlier that morning. I looked down at him; he looked beautiful laid there, ventilated but not moving.

I ran over to him and pressed my ear up against his sweet chest. I could hear his little heart beating against his chest wall. His fur was neatly groomed and he looked so peaceful. I kissed his face all over. "Please don't leave me, please don't leave me," I kept whispering to him over and over. My voice was frail and tired and my tears had made his ear wet. I could no longer cry silently to him. Before I knew it, the sound of my heartbreak was echoing around the vets. I couldn't control it.

"When you're ready," the vet said sympathetically. I felt Mum's hand on my shoulder. She leant forward and kissed Shabby on his head before exchanging a desperate look towards the vet. The room fell deathly silent. You could feel the love and heartbreak filling the space around us. I laid over

Shabby sobbing into his fur. I listened to his heart, savouring every beat until...

It stopped.

I was never going to hear this little heartbeat again. I was never going to feel his sweet, wet nose kiss my face again. I was never going to smell his beautiful fur.

Shabby, if love could have kept you here, you would've lived forever

Love at first sight.

This was Shabby the first day we met him.

Shabby looks lost

Brightly coloured buildings.

Sam cuddling Black Bear.

Dad enjoying English tea at Baileys Bar.

My brother, Sam enjoying the best cooked breakfast
on Sal (in his opinion.)

Shabby in OSPA's safe hands.

Shabby and Shanti as kennel buddies.

Shanti's rescue by OSPA.

Waiting for her forever home.

Journey home from Amsterdam

Much loved Shanti

22 hr 41 min (1,498 mi)

More like 80 hours travelling!!!

A thank you kiss from Shabby

Saying goodbye to Dada.

18th October 2018

Printed in Poland
by Amazon Fulfillment
Poland Sp. z o.o., Wrocław

49372891R00075